WHO, WHAT, WHY?

WHO WAS

MOSES?

CF4•K

DANIKA COOLEY

10 9 8 7 6 5 4 3 2 1
Copyright © Danika Cooley 2024
Paperback ISBN: 978-1-5271-1174-5
ebook ISBN: 978-1-5271-1239-1

Published by
Christian Focus Publications,
Geanies House, Fearn, Tain, Ross-shire,
IV20 1TW, Scotland, U.K.
www.christianfocus.com
email: info@christianfocus.com

Printed and bound by Bell and Bain, Glasgow

MIX
Paper | Supporting
responsible forestry
FSC® C007785

Cover design by Catriona Mackenzie
Illustrations by Martyn Smith

TABLE OF CONTENTS

Dedication

To the Reader (That's you!)
May you, too, know
our awesome God
face-to-face.

THE AUTHOR

Danika Cooley and her husband, Ed, are committed to leading their children to live for the glory of God. Danika has a passion for equipping parents to teach the Bible and Christian history to their kids. She is the author of *Help Your Kids Learn and Love the Bible*; *When Lightning Struck!: The Story of Martin Luther*; *Bible Investigators: Creation*; *Wonderfully Made: God's Story of Life from Conception to Birth*, and the *Who, What, Why?* Series about the history of our faith. Danika's three year Bible survey curriculum, Bible Road Trip™, is used by families around the world. Weekly, she encourages tens of thousands of parents to intentionally raise biblically literate children. Danika is a homeschool mother of four with a Bachelor of Arts degree from the University of Washington. Find her at ThinkingKidsBlog.org.

KNOWING
GOD FACE-TO-FACE

Long ago, in a land of pyramids and pharaohs, God's people—the Israelites—were slaves. They were forced to work tirelessly, building storehouse cities out of bricks made from mud and straw. This land, called Egypt, was ruled by a cruel Pharaoh and was the most powerful country of the ancient world.

Long before the time of our story, during a terrible famine—when no food grew for people to eat—Joseph, a son of Jacob, became second-in-command to the Pharaoh. You see, God gave Joseph a vision revealing a coming time of hunger, so, before disaster hit, Joseph stored up food in Egypt during several good years when food grew plentifully. This made Egypt a very wealthy and prosperous nation as people came to trade with them to avoid starvation.

During the famine, Joseph brought his father Jacob's family to Egypt: seventy-five people in all. The family of Jacob included Joseph's eleven brothers and their wives and children. The family settled in Egypt's

Nile Delta, the land of Goshen, where the Nile flows northward into the Mediterranean Sea.

Goshen was the perfect place for God's people to live. Just north of the Great Pyramids, the Nile River splits into several smaller rivers before dumping water into the sea all across the Delta. Each smaller river overflowed its banks yearly, enriching the surrounding land with dark soil from under the water and soaking the earth with life-giving water. This made Goshen a wonderful place for the shepherding Israelites to raise their cows, sheep, and goats.

God protected his people as their families grew in a land that was not their own. Nearly four hundred years passed in Egypt after the sons of Jacob moved to Goshen. The people of Israel multiplied until there were around two million men, women, and children. Sometime after Joseph's death a new Pharaoh who didn't remember Joseph or his father, Jacob came to power.

It was into this nation-within-a-nation that a baby was born. This wasn't just any baby, and he didn't grow up to be just any boy. No, this baby was born into the tribe of Levi—one of the sons of Jacob, which would become the tribe of God's priests. One day, this special child named Moses would know God face-to-face.

Some eighty years after his birth, God would call Moses to lead the Israelites out of slavery. The

Israelites would leave Egypt, travel through the hot desert wilderness, and learn to worship God properly at the mountain of Sinai. They would, in fact, live in the wilderness for forty years before God would lead them to the land he promised Jacob's grandfather, Abraham.

Throughout this time, Moses spoke to God often. God spoke to Moses, too. You see, in the time of the Old Testament, God spoke to kings and to ordinary people through his prophets—messengers he chose to speak his words. Moses was a special prophet of God. God used him to teach the Israelites about him and how to worship him.

Moses was born a Levite—part of the family of Jacob's son Levi. He was also born a slave. Later Moses became a special prophet and the leader of the Israelite nation. But what happened to him in between? After being born a slave he became a prince. Next, he was a vigilante—a person who takes the law into his own hands. After that, he was an outlaw—an exile running from the Pharaoh, king of Egypt. Whew!

Only after all that did God make Moses a prophet and the chosen leader of his people. God's Word—the Bible—tells us he was a prophet unlike any other. Deuteronomy 34:10 says, "And there has not arisen a prophet since in Israel like Moses, whom the LORD knew face to face." Through Moses, the Lord worked mighty signs and wonders so that all the world would know that he is the one and only God.

Scripture mentions Moses nearly seven hundred times—and God still speaks to us through Moses. You see, today God speaks through his Word, the Bible. The books of the Bible: Genesis, Exodus, Leviticus, Numbers, and Deuteronomy, are all written by Moses. These books are also called the Pentateuch which means "five books" in the Greek language. Though Moses was the human author of the Pentateuch, God was the divine author. Moses wrote what God told him to, in his own words and with his own personality—just as Moses spoke to God's people, the Israelites, as a prophet.

As you read on you will discover more about this humble man of faith and courage. He knew God face-to-face, trusted, and talked to him. So remember that you, too, can talk to God anytime. After all, in Philippians 4:6, the Bible tells us: "Do not be anxious about anything, but in everything by prayer and supplication with thanksgiving let your requests be made known to God."

GREATER THAN TREASURE

Hebrews 11:24-26 says, "By faith Moses, when he was grown up, refused to be called the son of Pharaoh's daughter, choosing rather to be mistreated with the people of God than to enjoy the fleeting pleasures of sin. He considered the reproach of Christ greater wealth than the treasures of Egypt, for he was looking to the reward."

As an adopted prince, Moses had a life full of wealth and pleasure. However, he left the palace and suffered

for the Israelites, which should remind us of how Jesus suffered for his people. Moses cared more about eternal life with God than temporary riches on earth The Old Testament believers trusted God's promise to send a Messiah who would save them from their sins. Jesus is far greater than any earthly treasure.

RESCUED!

Now, in the land of Egypt, there were grand palaces with giant statues of pharaohs who ruled before. Towering pyramids held elaborate mazes leading to kingly burial chambers. Egypt was a place of learning where people wrote in pictures, called hieroglyphs, that stood for letters, sounds, or sometimes words. Dentists and doctors put fillings in teeth, set broken bones, diagnosed cancer, and even performed basic brain surgery.

The land was also a place of false worship, where the people followed fake gods they thought looked like bulls, cows, frogs, and even the sun. In fact, each pharaoh believed he was the god of the sun, born into human flesh. Many of the people of Israel also followed the idols of Egypt. This is something the true God, Yahweh, hates—the worship of creatures, statues, and people.

There were, though, Israelites who loved the God of Abraham, Isaac, and Jacob, who is the living and mighty God whom Christians serve today. Among the true believers was a man named Amram and his wife Jochebed. Both from the tribe of Levi, which would later be dedicated to God as priests and worship leaders. They had three children. Their oldest, Miriam, was probably around your age when Moses was born. Aaron was just three years old when Moses entered the world.

By the time Moses was born, the Pharaoh was worried that the people of Israel would fight back against the Egyptians. You see, Pharaoh forced the

Israelite people to work as slaves under the hot sun. The Pharaoh also decided that all Israelite baby boys must die. That was a wicked, evil decision.

Pharaoh told two Israelite midwives—ladies who help women deliver their babies—to kill baby boys as they were born. The midwives, named Shiphrah and Puah, loved God, so they did not kill any babies at all. Pharaoh roared, "Why did you let the little boys live?"

"Israelite women are stronger than Egyptian women," they replied. "They don't need help giving birth! We weren't there to see any babies born."

Though Shiphrah and Puah lied to Pharaoh, they honored God by saving the lives of many children. So, God blessed the women with their own families. He blessed his people, the Israelites, by causing them to multiply and grow as a nation.

Pharaoh was still afraid of God's people, so he ordered Egyptians to throw Israelite infant boys into the Nile—and the Egyptians did it. It is a terrible

act to kill a defenseless child. Pharaoh's order was exceedingly wicked.

It was into this world that little Moses was born to Amram and Jochebed. They loved their beautiful little boy, and they had faith in the Lord God, so they hid Moses in their home for three months. Now, as babies grow, their lungs get stronger, and their cries get louder. As Moses cried louder and louder, Jochebed realized she could no longer hide her precious baby.

She feared God, not the Pharaoh, but she had Miriam and Aaron to protect as well.

So, Jochebed went down to the Nile and picked some bulrushes—tall grass that grows along the banks—and wove a little basket with a lid. Next, she heated tar, coating the inside of her little basket to make it waterproof. It must have been difficult for Jochebed to place little Moses in the basket she made, leaving him to float along the banks of a giant river full of crocodiles. But, Jochebed trusted God to care for Moses.

Jochebed left her daughter, Miriam, hiding in the tall Nile grass, watching to see what would happen to her baby brother. Miriam hid until she saw the Princess of Egypt come to the Nile to bathe. When the basket was opened, there was little Moses crying with his great big lungs. Even though Pharaoh's daughter knew that Moses was an Israelite baby, and that her father had ordered all those baby boys to be killed, she decided to keep him.

Now, Miriam was a wise girl, and she knew Pharaoh's daughter had no way to feed little Moses. After all, babies drink milk from their mothers. So, she rushed to ask Pharaoh's daughter if she needed an Israelite woman to nurse the baby for her.

That is how Jochebed nursed and raised her own son through his toddler years before returning him to the Pharaoh's daughter at the palace. It is how Moses spent his early years learning to love God, learning the Hebrew language, and getting to know his older sister and brother, Miriam and Aaron. Moses spent the first forty years of his life as a prince in the most educated, wealthiest nation on earth.

Perhaps this is where an ordinary story would end. But there is nothing ordinary about this story. Moses grew to know about the Lord God—whom his parents loved and served. God would one day call Moses to be the man who knew him face-to-face. God was arranging the events of Moses' life in a way that would prepare him to be God's faithful servant.

EGYPTIAN WISDOM

Acts 7:20-22 says, "At this time Moses was born; and he was beautiful in God's sight. And he was brought up for three months in his father's house, and when he was exposed, Pharaoh's daughter adopted him and brought him up as her own son. And Moses was instructed in all the wisdom of the Egyptians, and he was mighty in his words and deeds."

God arranged for Moses to grow up in the palaces of Egypt. There, Moses would have learned to write, to structure treaties and laws, and to command armies at war. Moses was trained in the skills he needed in order to lead the Israelites, to prepare them to fight for the land of Canaan, and to write five books of the Bible.

FORTY YEARS
OF EXILE

When Moses was forty years old he chose to be with his people rather than continue a life of princely ease. While visiting the enslaved Israelites, Moses saw an Egyptian beating an Israelite. Now, Moses was Egyptian royalty. He could have spoken to the Egyptian, or appealed to Pharaoh. Moses certainly should have prayed to God. Instead, he killed the man and buried him in the sand. What an atrocious sin!

The following day, Moses tried to reason with two Israelites who were fighting. "You aren't our prince." One of the men declared, "Will you kill me, too?" Moses realized he could not hide his sin—from Pharaoh or from God.

So Moses fled Egypt, all the way to the wilderness of Sinai in the land of Midian. Some Midianites dwelled in walled cities, while others camped in the desert, caring for sheep and goats. Our exiled prince finally came to a well where seven Midianite sisters tried to water their sheep, but other shepherds chased them away. Moses defended the girls, drawing water for their sheep. When they told their father about this he asked, "Why didn't you invite this man to dinner? Go get him!"

Moses lived in Jethro's camp and married one of the sisters, Zipporah. They had a son named Gershom— which means "sojourner—a traveler or stranger," because Moses was far from home. They had another

son, Eliezer—which means "my God is my helper," because God saved Moses from Pharaoh's anger.

Our story speeds forward again until Moses is eighty years old. Watching sheep in the desert must have been humbling for our former prince. Yet, Moses

became a caring shepherd who knew the wilderness of Sinai well.

One day, Moses was on Mount Sinai—also called Horeb—when he saw a bush on fire, but not burning up. Naturally, Moses walked over to see what was going on. That's when he heard God call him, right out of the middle of the bush, "Moses, Moses!"

Moses said, "Here I am."

God told Moses to take his sandals off, because he was standing on holy ground. In Egypt, everyone removed their footwear in the Pharaoh's court as a sign of respect. So, it was especially important that Moses remove his shoes while appearing before the King of the Universe.

"I am the God of your father, the God of Abraham, the God of Isaac, and the God of Jacob," God said. Moses was afraid, so he hid his face.

God had promised Moses' ancestor, Abraham, that he would make Abraham's descendants as numerous as the stars in the heavens, rescue his people from slavery, punish their oppressors, bring them out of a foreign land with many riches, and give them the land of Canaan. God was going to keep his promises. Not only that, Moses was going to be his prophet before Pharaoh. After leaving Egypt, God promised that Moses would serve him right here on the mountain of Sinai.

However, Moses did not want the job! He did not want to go to the elders of Israel. He did not want to talk to Pharaoh! "What if the elders ask me for your name?" he said to God.

God replied, "Yahweh" which means "I AM WHO I AM." God instructed Moses to tell the Israelites that he is the LORD, the God of Abraham, Isaac, and Jacob. God said this is his name forever. God is the Creator of the heavens and the earth. He always has been, he is, and he always will be. Only God is God.

Moses still did not want to go, so he argued with God. First, Moses said the Israelite elders and the Egyptians would not believe God sent him. So, God gave Moses signs to do in front of them. Moses threw his staff to the ground where it turned into a snake. Then he caught it by the tail and it returned to being a staff. God told Moses to put his hand inside his cloak. When he took it out, his hand was white with a disease called leprosy. After he put it back inside his cloak, his hand was healed.

Next, Moses argued he could not speak well. God replied that he made Moses' mouth. God promised to teach Moses what to speak. Finally, Moses said,

"Please, Lord, send someone else." That made God angry. He said he would send Moses' brother Aaron to see Pharaoh with Moses. Finally Moses obeyed.

Moses traveled to Egypt with his wife, Zipporah, and their sons. His brother Aaron met them at Mount Sinai. Together, Moses and Aaron told the elders of Israel all of God's words, showed the signs God gave them, and the people believed. They all worshiped God, the great I AM.

GOD'S HOUSE

In the Bible, we are told that Moses was a servant in God's house, serving the Israelites. Hebrews 3:1-6 explains that the Church—God's chosen people—is like a house.

Why does the Bible use the word house? What does that mean?

It sounds a bit strange at first, but the Bible uses picture language like this so we can understand God's truths.

The following verses in Hebrews 3:5-6 tell us the most amazing fact about God's house. It says, "Now Moses was faithful in all God's house as a servant, to testify to the things that were to be spoken later, but Christ is faithful over God's house as a son. And we are his house, if indeed we hold fast our confidence and our boasting in our hope."

God is telling us that Jesus Christ is the head of the church. Jesus, the Son of God, is the builder of the house. He is the builder of the church!

What a wonderful thing to follow him!

OUT OF EGYPT

Moses walked into Pharaoh's throne room with his brother, Aaron. God's message was, "Let my people go that they may hold a feast to me in the wilderness." Pharaoh scoffed, "Who is this God? I don't know him, and I won't let his people go!"

This was no surprise to God. Before Moses visited Pharaoh, God announced he would harden Pharaoh's heart so the Egyptian king would not let God's people go. Remember, the people of ancient Egypt worshiped many false gods. But, our great God, Yahweh, is the only true God. God hardened the wicked Pharaoh's heart so that God's glory would be seen by the Israelites, the Egyptians, and their neighbors.

God showed his glory by inflicting ten plagues on Egypt, one right after the other. A plague is a terrible disease, affliction, or hardship. Each plague was a judgment by God on the wickedness of the Egyptian people. The plagues also showed how powerless Egypt's fake "gods" truly were.

First, the Nile turned to blood for a week. Then, frogs and more frogs filled the land of Egypt. Next, God sent swarming gnats. Then, flies were everywhere— except in Goshen, where God's people lived. Still, the Pharaoh's heart was hard. So, God sent a plague to kill their livestock. Then there were boils—horrible, painful sores all over the Egyptians. Next, hail killed the animals and people in the fields. After the hail,

God sent locusts that ate all the grain, trees, and vegetables. Then, there was pitch black darkness for three days straight. Still, Pharaoh would not let God's people go. Finally, God warned Pharaoh of a terrifying plague that left all of Egypt wailing in tears.

God had Moses prepare his people for the Exodus—coming out of Egypt. Their Egyptian neighbors gave

them clothing, silver, gold, and jewelry. Then, each family sacrificed a perfect lamb, painting the doorframe of their home with the lamb's blood. They ate roasted lamb, unleavened bread, and bitter herbs wearing their sandals and holding staffs—ready to go.

At midnight, every Egyptian family found their firstborn son dead. But, the homes of the Israelites were passed over by the Lord when he came across the blood of the lamb. Moses and Aaron quickly led the people of Israel out of Egypt in the middle of the night. They followed God's glory, which shone in a pillar

of cloud during the day and a pillar of fire at night. It led them to the edge of the wilderness, between Egypt and the Red Sea.

Now, Pharaoh—who lost his son, too—set out after the Israelites. The people saw the armies of Egypt coming, with horses galloping and chariot wheels kicking up dust. "Why did you bring us here to die?" they wailed at Moses.

Moses trusted that God had a plan. He told them not to fear, but to wait for God's salvation. "The LORD will fight for you, and you have only to be silent."

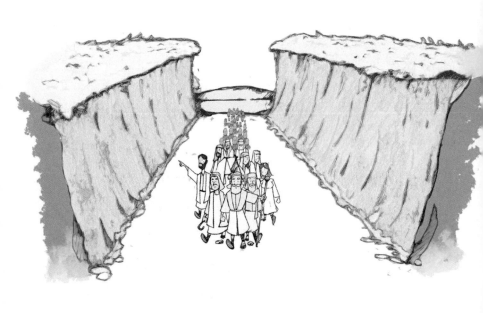

The Lord did fight for his people. Moses stretched his hand out over the Red Sea—and the waters split in half. God's people walked right through the sea on dry land. Of course, the Egyptians charged after the Israelites. Once all the people of God reached the shore, God told Moses to hold out his hand again, and the waters closed over the Egyptian army. Moses and the people praised our amazing God with a song and the women danced with tambourines.

Just three days later, though, the complaining, whining, and grumbling really started. First, the people came to bitter, undrinkable water. Moses prayed to God, threw a log into the water, and God made the water sweet. Again, the people complained. They were hungry, and angry about it. Moses trusted God, who sent quail that evening, and six days each week there was bread from heaven on the ground—called manna.

Again, God's people complained about water. Moses was angry, and he worried they might kill him. "What should I do with this people?" he asked God. God told Moses to strike a rock with his staff. Water flowed out of the rock, enough for everyone to drink.

When Amalekite fighters attacked the people on the edges of the procession, Moses had his young helper, Joshua, lead the Israelite men into battle the very next day. Moses, Aaron, and their friend, Hur, all stood on top of a hill during the great fight. Moses, of course, prayed. He knew only God could help the Israelites win the battle against their fierce desert foes.

While Moses was praying, he held up his hand. When Moses' hand was up, the people of Israel were winning the battle. Whenever Moses was tired and lowered his arm, the Amalekites began to win. So, eighty-year-old Moses sat on a rock while Aaron and Hur stood beside him holding up his arms until the sun set. The people of Israel defeated the people of Amalek because the Lord helped them.

GOD HEARS OUR CRY

Moses always cried out to God when he encountered trouble, and God answered his prayers. The Israelites also cried out to God from Egypt. Exodus 2:23b-24 says, "Their cry for rescue from slavery came up to God. And God heard their groaning, and God remembered his covenant with Abraham, with Isaac, and with Jacob." God saw his people and acted on their behalf.

In Micah 6:4, God says through his prophet, Micah, "For I brought you up from the land of Egypt and redeemed you from the house of slavery, and I sent before you Moses, Aaron, and Miriam." God answered the prayers of his people. It is wonderful news that he hears and answers your prayers, too!

THE MOUNTAIN
OF GOD

After the battle with the Amalekites, God led Moses and the people to Mount Sinai, where Yahweh had appeared in the burning bush. It was time for the ragtag group to become an organized nation led by Yahweh. So, God gave them laws to help them love him and love each other. He taught Moses how to structure their government. God gave Moses plans for building a tabernacle—a portable temple—so the people could worship him correctly.

Moses spoke to the elders, telling them God had established a covenant. A covenant is a legal contract that binds two sets of people together. The people of Israel were to promise to keep God's commandments, and God promised to make Israel his holy nation. The elders of Israel agreed to follow God's laws. Then, God told the people to spend three days preparing to stand before him, ceremonially clean according to God's rules.

Moses set up markers all along the base of the mountain to prevent people from going too far. The mountain was a holy place, and anyone coming too close without permission would die. After three days, a tremendous trumpet blast sounded louder and louder from a thick cloud on top of Mount Sinai. Thunder rumbled and lightning flashed. There was fire, smoke, and the whole mountain shook like an earthquake.

Moses spoke to the Lord, and God's answers sounded like thunder. The people shook before the Lord in fear because his awesome presence was terrifying to them. Moses went up to see God, and God gave Moses the Ten Commandments. The mountain still thundered and smoked, with trumpet blasts coming from the cloud. The people were terrified of God's glory.

God gave Moses many additional laws, called the Book of the Covenant. Then, he promised Moses he would help the Israelites fight the people of the land of Canaan—the land God had promised to Abraham. The Canaanites hated God, and they worshiped idols. All land belongs to God, so it was his to give or to take away.

Next, Moses led Aaron and his sons, along with seventy elders of Israel, up the mountain to see God. Now, no human can survive seeing all God's glory, so God showed them the floor of heaven under his feet, which was paved with something like sapphire. Then, they ate and drank in God's presence. Moses told the elders to wait on the mountainside for him. For forty days and forty nights, Moses was on the mountaintop with God in a cloud of burning fire.

Below the mountain, a throng of people demanded Aaron make idols for them. They did not know where Moses had gone, and they did not know where God was. That was silly, since they could look up Mount Sinai and see the fiery cloud. In fact, the elders had just eaten with God! Now, Aaron knew the Lord, and he had been with Moses throughout the Exodus. Still, Aaron made a golden calf from earrings donated by the people. The Israelites worshiped the calf, holding a wicked festival.

God knows all things, and he knew the people were worshiping a gold idol. He told Moses he was going to destroy the Israelites and start over with a nation

descended from Moses! Though the people of Israel were grumblers, Moses asked God to spare them. As Moses and Joshua descended the mountain, Moses saw people dancing and hollering in front of the golden calf. He threw the stone tablets of the law on the ground, breaking them. Then, he set fire to the calf, ground it to powder, and made the people drink water mixed with burnt gold.

The punishment for their sin—death—was a hard judgment from God. Moses had the Levites, who still served God alone, kill the idolators with their swords. Around three thousand people died. Then, God sent a plague on the people.

After that disaster, Moses wanted to see God— not his feet, or his cloud, or fire in a bush, but God himself. The Lord explained that no one could see God and live. So, God placed Moses in a crack in the mountain and covered him with his hand. Yahweh passed by, proclaiming, "The LORD, the LORD, a God merciful and gracious, slow to anger, and abounding in steadfast love and faithfulness, keeping steadfast love for thousands" (Exodus 34:6-7). After that, Moses' face glowed from the glory of the Lord. In fact, he had to wear a veil for a time so that his face would not frighten the people.

God wrote the Ten Commandments on new tablets of stone that Moses made, and Moses had the people celebrate the Passover feast to remember how Yahweh had saved them in Egypt. The pillar of cloud lifted from the tabernacle, and the people gathered their tents and belongings. After the Levites packed up the tabernacle, the people followed the Lord toward their new home, never knowing how long they would camp at each spot. Sometimes it was just a night, sometimes it was months.

THE LAW POINTS TO JESUS

Jesus taught that Scripture points to him. He said that if we love God, we will come to Jesus to receive life. Then, in John 5:46-47, he said, "For if you believed Moses, you would believe me; for he wrote of me. But if you do not believe his writings, how will you believe my words?"

Moses wrote about our need for forgiveness through Jesus when he recorded God's law, which all people break. He wrote of Jesus, the perfect Lamb of God, when he wrote the story of the Passover—with a lamb sacrificed to spare the people from death. Moses recorded God's instructions for the tabernacle and for worship, which points to Jesus according to Hebrews 8:1-2 which says, "Now the point in what we are saying is this: we have such a high priest, one who is seated at the right hand of the throne of the Majesty in heaven, a minister in the holy places, in the true tent that the Lord set up, not man."

GRUMBLING
IN THE WILDERNESS

After witnessing God's ten plagues in Egypt, crossing the Red Sea on dry land, and eating bread from heaven, the people should have praised God for all his blessings. But, the people of Israel forgot to be grateful for anything. As they marched for three days toward Kadesh on the southern border of Canaan, they grumbled, whined, and complained. Walking to the Promised Land was hard, they said. God was angry at their grumpy hearts, so a fire spread at the edge of camp. When the people cried out to Moses for help, he prayed to God and the fire went out.

Still, the people stood at their tent doors and wailed. They didn't want bread from heaven anymore. No, they wanted fish, cucumber, melon, and leeks, like they ate in Egypt. Now both God and Moses were angry.

God announced there would be so much meat that it would come out their noses! Quail flew into the camp on a wind God brought from the sea. The wailing people dried their tears and spent two days catching the fat little birds. Imagine a pickup truck so full of quail that it mounds above the bed. That's how many quail each family killed! The people were stuffing their faces with meat when God sent a terrible plague.

Once the greedy people were buried, the Lord led the Israelites to a place called Hazeroth. There, Miriam and Aaron complained about Moses' wife. Then they whined, "Why is Moses the leader of Israel? God speaks through us, too!" So, God called Aaron, Miriam, and Moses to stand before him at the tabernacle. God declared that he spoke to humble and faithful Moses face-to-face. "Why then were you not afraid to speak against my servant Moses?" When God left them, Miriam's skin was white with a terrible disease called leprosy. Aaron confessed their sin, and Moses asked God to heal Miriam. God did, but Miriam had to stay outside the camp for seven days.

Next, the people camped at a large oasis just south of the Promised Land. Moses assembled a man from each Israelite tribe to spy on Canaan. His helper, Joshua, went as the chief of the tribe of Ephraim. Moses told the twelve spies to bring a report. "Are the Canaanites strong? Do they have good gardens and trees? Bring back some fruit," he told them.

Forty days later, the spies returned with a giant cluster of grapes carried by two men. They lugged pomegranates and figs. "The land flows with milk and honey," the spies said, "But, we saw the sons of Anak! They were huge, and we were like grasshoppers. The massive cities have tall walls."

"Hold on," said Caleb of Judah as the people cried out in fear. "We should attack right away! We are stronger than the people in the land." Joshua, too, argued that the people should enter the land. After all, God was with them!

But, the people did not trust God. Instead, they wept, wailed, and grumbled yet again. They were so angry with Moses and Aaron, they wanted to stone them! This time, God was angry. The grumblers refused to enter the land God was giving them. "How long will this people despise me?" God asked. "And how long will they not believe in me?" Moses asked God for mercy—again. So, God announced he would let everyone live, but anyone age twenty or older would die before Israel entered the Promised Land.

Rather than repent and worship God, the people decided to attack the land of Canaan. "Don't do it!" said Moses. "God is no longer with you." They attacked anyway, without Moses and without God. They lost the battle—badly.

Korah, Dathan, and Abiram, all Levites, gathered two hundred and fifty chiefs to grumble some more, "We should be the leaders." God had Moses call the grumblers to hold incense censers before God at the tabernacle, but Dathan and Abiram refused to come. As the two men stood with their families at the door of their tents, the ground swallowed them, and everything they owned. Korah's animals, and family, too, were swallowed by the earth. At the tabernacle, fire came from the Lord and burnt up Korah and his 250 men.

Now, the grumbling stopped. Right? No! "You killed God's people," the Israelites said to Moses and Aaron. Again, Moses prayed for mercy. While God sent a plague, Moses told Aaron to stand with an offering, a censer of incense, between the living and the dead—more than fourteen thousand people had already died. The plague from God ended.

Then, God had Moses instruct each head of the twelve tribes of Israel, including Aaron, to write their name on their staff. They left the staffs in the tabernacle overnight where Aaron's staff sprouted leaves, flowers, and almonds. Moses showed the people that the Lord chose Aaron as the High Priest. Instead of worshiping God, they cried that they would all die.

CHARACTER MATTERS

Numbers 12:3 says, "Now the man Moses was very meek, more than all people who were on the face of the earth." Verses 6-7 state that rather than appearing to Moses in dreams or visions, God spoke to Moses clearly, face-to-face. Moses, God said, "is faithful in all my house."

A meek—or humble—person is not concerned about their own importance, but about honoring the Lord. A faithful person is loyal to God, worshiping God alone. The Bible highlights Moses' character—the qualities he possessed as a person—because how we live for God is important. If you love Jesus and repent of your sins, God will grow your endurance and character, and your hope in Jesus. (Read Romans 5:1-5!)

HEADED TO
THE PROMISED LAND

The people came to Meribah where they quarreled with Moses and with the Lord. "We would rather be dead like our brothers—Korah, Dathan, Abiram, and the elders!" they whined. "Why did you bring us to this evil place? There is no water for us!" I'm sure you're thinking, "Oh no! The people have called the place God brought them to 'evil'!" Moses and Aaron felt the same way. The brothers fell on their faces before the glory of God at the tabernacle.

God told Moses to have all the people gather before a rock, hold his staff, and tell the rock to give the people water. Well, that's not at all what Moses did. Instead, Moses and Aaron stood in front of the people. "You rebels, should we bring water out of the rock for you?" Moses cried. Uh oh! When he used the word "we" Moses told the people he and Aaron were going to give them water, not God. Then, Moses struck the rock twice. Uh oh, again!

Lots and lots of water gushed out of the rock. But Moses never spoke to the rock like God told him to. God told Moses and Aaron they would never set foot in the Promised Land. They had not believed God, nor shown him to be holy.

Israel asked the country of Edom if they could travel the King's Highway on the way to the Promised Land. Even though Edom and Israel were related by a common ancestor, Edom refused. In fact, the Edomites attacked Israelite stragglers. So, Moses led the people the long way around Edom.

Moses' brother, Aaron, died and his son Eleazar was made the High Priest. Miriam had died just before the debacle at Meribah. As the people of Israel camped on the Plains of Moab, God began to prepare them to enter the Promised Land. There were battles and victories, and later there were speeches and promises.

First the Israelites fought the king of Arad and destroyed his cities. Then, they warred against King Sihon of the Amorites. Next, they conquered King Og of Bashan. The people of these countries hated the true God, Yahweh. So, God took their land and gave it to the Israelites.

The Israelites were busy fighting and they were busy complaining. They even said they hated manna from heaven, which they called "worthless food." This time, God sent poisonous serpents. Many died before the people confessed they had sinned. God had Moses make a bronze serpent and raise it up on a pole for people to look at. Now, this seems like a strange way for God to save people. After all, the people were not allowed to make or worship idols. Perhaps God

was showing the people a picture of their ugly sin, reminding them that our sins are like snake venom— sin is deadly. About 1,400 years later, when Jesus Christ was crucified on a cross, he died for the sin of all who turn away from the deadly venom of their sin to him.

When God's people camped along the Jordan River, across from Jericho, kings throughout Moab and Canaan began to worry. News carried quickly in

the cities and towns, and soon everyone knew God had given the Israelites victory over the Amorite kings. Balak, King of Moab, hired a sorcerer to curse God's people, sending messengers to the false prophet, Balaam.

That night, God appeared to Balaam in a dream and told him not to go with the men because the Israelites were blessed. Again, Balak sent men to Balaam and again, God appeared to Balaam. Even so, Balaam set out on his donkey because his true love was money, not God. Balaam did not see the angel of the Lord standing in the road with his sword drawn, but his donkey did.

The donkey went into the field, so Balaam hit her. Later, Balaam's donkey saw the angel of the Lord between two narrow walls, so she smashed Balaam's foot against a wall. Balaam hit her again. The next time, the angel of the Lord stood in a narrow place, so the donkey laid down. Balaam beat her with his staff. The donkey spoke, "What did I do to you? You hit me three times!"

Balaam was so irate, he wasn't even surprised. "You made a fool out of me! If I had a sword, I would kill you," he said.

The donkey replied, "Have I ever treated you like this before?"

Balaam said, "No." Then, God allowed him to see the angel of the Lord holding a sword.

The angel explained that if the donkey had not saved Balaam, he would have killed Balaam with the sword. Balaam confessed to the angel of the Lord that he had sinned. The angel told him to speak only the words he gave him.

King Balak hired Balaam to curse Israel. Instead, Balaam blessed God's people, not once but seven times. Now, the nations in Canaan and on the east side of the Jordan River knew they were in trouble. Still, they did not repent. Moses must have felt encouraged by the account of Balaam's blessings which God had him write.

THE BEST PROMISE OF ALL

In Acts 26:22-23, Paul said, "To this day I have had the help that comes from God, and so I stand here testifying both to small and great, saying nothing but what the prophets and Moses said would come to pass: that the Christ must suffer and that, by being the first to rise from the dead, he would proclaim light both to our people and to the Gentiles."

All of Scripture points to Jesus. We have all sinned and broken God's law. That is horribly sad, because the penalty for sin is death. But, God had a wonderful plan for salvation. Jesus lived a perfect, sinless life. Then, he was crucified, taking the penalty for all who repent. Those who believe in the risen Jesus will spend eternity with him.

A BIG SPEECH

Eventually, the adults who left Egypt during the Exodus died, one by one. Finally, only Moses, Joshua, and Caleb remained from the adults who had left Egypt. Moses was 120 years old.

Though it takes only eleven days to walk from Mount Sinai to Kadesh, the people of Israel spent over forty years in the desert wilderness, training to be a nation chosen by Yahweh. They learned how to worship God, they constructed the tabernacle according to God's instructions, and they learned how God wanted them to treat others.

The people, too, had proven themselves to be terribly whiny whiners. They complained about everything the Lord gave them. They even grumbled about bread from heaven. Even while he disciplined them, God showed great mercy by not wiping out the people that complained against him. Through it all, there was Moses, leading the people of God while he spoke to the Lord face-to-face.

Moses was a prophet—a man who spoke the words of God to the people. He was one of the authors of God's Word—God gave Moses the words to write down for the Israelites, and now us, to read. He was a military commander—he helped lead the people of Israel into battle against people who did not love God. He was also a man who prayed—he prayed for mercy for the people when they sinned, and he asked God to meet their needs.

Now, as Moses stood on the Plains of Moab at the edge of the Promised Land, he looked out over the men, women, and children who had grown up in the desert. In three long speeches, Moses spoke the words God gave him to help prepare the Israelites to enter Canaan.

In his first speech, Moses helped the people look back. He reviewed the history of Israel's journey

through the wilderness and their response to God. What kind of events did he remind the people about? Israel had refused to enter Canaan when Caleb and Joshua said it was good and Moses urged them to trust God. Instead, they listened to ten frightened spies. Because of their disobedience, the people wandered in the wilderness, led by the glory of God for thirty-eight years. Then, God gave them the victory over Kings Sihon and Og. Moses talked about his own sin, too, which barred him from crossing the Jordan River into the land of Canaan. Because Moses could not go to the Promised Land, Joshua would guide the people of Israel. He reminded the Israelites that only God should be worshiped.

In his second speech, Moses urged the people to look up to the Lord. He wanted them to think about God and their relationship with him. Moses reminded the Israelites about the law God gave them—rules about how to honor God and rules about loving others in a way that is pleasing to God. "Hear, O Israel," he said in Deuteronomy 6:4-5, "The LORD our God, the LORD is one. You shall love the LORD your God with all your heart and with all your soul and with all your might." We should love God with everything we have. Moses also told parents to teach their children about the Lord and his commands at all times—when they sit, walk, lie down, and wake up. We should always look up to the God who made us and praise him!

In his third speech, Moses pointed the people forward. He wanted them to think about the future, and how they should serve God faithfully in their new land. God would curse the people if they disobeyed him, but they would be blessed if they obeyed his commands. Then, God directed the people, through Moses, to set up and plaster large stones on Mount Ebal—in the land of Canaan over the Jordan. In the plaster, they were to write the words God gave them. Then, half the tribes were to stand on Mount Gerizim, while the other six tribes would stand on Mount Ebal

facing Mount Gerazim, over the town of Shechem. The mountains are very close to each other at one point, so the people could hear one another. Then, the Levites—the tribe of priests—were to declare curses in the direction of Mount Ebal for different kinds of disobedience. After each declaration, all the people would say, "Amen." Because Moses could not enter Canaan, Joshua led this ceremony.

Standing in Moab, Moses once more reminded the people of the covenant they made with God.

They would follow his commands, and they would be his people. Moses told them that when they disobeyed God, they must remember the bad things that would happen—the curses—because they turned away from the Lord their God. But, when they returned to God, he would have mercy on them and forgive them. "See," Moses said at the end of his third speech in Deuteronomy 30:15, "I have set before you today life and good, death and evil."

The choice God gave his people was clear. If they chose the goodness of dwelling with God, then God would bless them in the land of Canaan.

THE WORK OF OUR HANDS

Did you know that Moses also wrote Psalm 90? In this Psalm, Moses praises God, who is everlasting— he has always been and always will be. Humans live sometimes seventy or eighty years. But, for God a thousand years is like a day is for us. In Psalm 90:12, Moses says to God, "So teach us to number our days that we may get a heart of wisdom."

One day, God will judge unbelievers for their sins. We should remember that we are only here for a short time. We will spend the rest of eternity either with God, or apart from him. It is a gift that we can trust in Jesus as our Savior, knowing that we will spend forever with God because our sins are forgiven.

EDGE OF THE
PROMISED LAND

Moses had just one last set of speeches for the people. He led the Israelites through the wilderness for forty years, praying for them even when they were hard to govern. Moses must have felt a little emotional about leaving them.

First, Moses reassured them they would live in the Promised Land. God himself would give them the victory. Joshua, would be their new leader. To the people, Moses said, "Be strong and courageous." God would be with them. To Joshua he said, "Be strong and courageous." The Lord God would go with him.

Next, Moses called the priests before him and told them to read God's Word—the Book of the Law that God had Moses write—to the people every seven years. The priests were to read Scripture to all the people, to the men, the women, the little children, and the people of other nations living with them. It was important, Moses said, that the children learned to fear God through hearing his Word.

Then, Moses wrote a long song for the people to sing. His hymn taught the people that God is great. The Lord is faithful, just, and without sin. But, the song said, the people were sinful, rebelling against their Father God who created them. Still, God chose his people and gave them an inheritance in the Promised Land. God was with his people in the desert even though they dishonored God and served idols. God allowed them to do this because these false gods would not save them. He sent disasters to turn the people of Israel back to him: fire, plagues, snakes and swords. But God showed mercy to his servants, disciplining them rather than destroying them. We must learn too, that idols are false but that our God is very real!

After Moses and Joshua had sung this special song in front of all Israel, Moses then told the people to take his words to heart and teach them to their children. He wanted the children of Israel to know God and obey him so that all would go well with them. Finally, Moses blessed each Israelite tribe.

When Moses finished his great big speech to the people of Israel, he left them and visited with God one last time on earth, face-to-face. Now, Moses was going to die, but he would spend eternity face-to-face

with the Lord God, Yahweh. That is because Moses loved God and he followed him, repenting of his sins. So, Moses climbed from the plains of Moab to the top of Mount Nebo, which is across the Jordan River from the walled city of Jericho in Canaan.

Even at the age of 120, Moses was still strong, with healthy eyes and good vision. God had blessed Moses with all he needed to serve the Lord. From the top of the mountain, the Lord God showed Moses all of the land he would soon give to his people. It was the same

land that God had promised to Abraham, Isaac, and Jacob. God always, always keeps his promises, because he is faithful. God reminded Moses one last time that he could not set foot in the land of Canaan because he had dishonored the Lord in front of the people of Israel, not treating him as holy.

Moses died in the land of Moab, but the Bible tells us something quite extraordinary. It says that God himself buried Moses in the valley in Moab. No one knows where Moses' grave is, except for God.

The very end of the book of Deuteronomy, in 34:10-12, says, "And there has not arisen a prophet since in Israel like Moses, whom the LORD knew face to face, none like him for all the signs and the wonders that the LORD sent him to do in the land of Egypt, to Pharaoh and to all his servants and to all his land, and for all the mighty power and all the great deeds of terror that Moses did in the sight of all Israel."

Moses was a great man in history, not because he was a mighty king or warrior, but because he loved and served God. The Lord blessed Moses, not with riches or fine foods, but with his presence. Moses was a servant-hearted man who spoke, and wrote, God's words for all who follow the Lord, so that we may better know how to love and worship God, and how to love other people.

You will probably never see an event like the plagues on Egypt, or follow God's presence in a pillar of cloud and fire through the wilderness. Still, there is a lot we can learn from Moses, the prophet who knew God face-to-face. We can follow Moses' example by loving God with all our heart, mind, and soul. We can love others by serving them the way Moses cared for the Israelites. We can know God, as Moses did, by praying to him as the Bible tells us to in Philippians 4:6, "Do not be anxious about anything, but in everything by prayer and supplication with thanksgiving let your requests be made known to God."

LIFE EVERLASTING

God gave the apostle John an amazing vision, which John recorded in Revelation 15:3-4. It is about the people of God worshiping before his throne with harps:

"And they sing the song of Moses, the servant of God, and the song of the Lamb, saying,

'Great and amazing are your deeds,

O Lord God the Almighty!

Just and true are your ways,

O King of the nations!

Who will not fear, O Lord,

and glorify your name?

For you alone are holy.

All nations will come

and worship you,

for your righteous acts have been revealed.'"

God's deeds truly are great and amazing—he is the Almighty Lord. Everyone who believes in Jesus—the Lamb of God—and turns from their sins will one day sing the song of Moses and the song of the Lamb. Christians will have life everlasting!

TIMELINE

Note: The dating for the rule of Pharaohs in Ancient Egypt varies, as calendars varied. Also, there are two widely accepted dates for the Exodus. This timeline is based on the early date. The early date of the Exodus works backward from dates in Scripture, and is supported by many conservative scholars. Today, biblical scholars are still not entirely certain who the Pharaoh of the Exodus is.

c. 3000 BC

Egypt unites, and Memphis is built on the boundary of the two to unite Egypt. The city was the capital of the Old Kingdom.

c. 2630 BC

The first pyramid, the Step Pyramid, is built in Saqqara, Egypt by Pharaoh Djoser. It takes twenty years to build.

c. 2560 BC

Pharaoh Khufu builds the Great Pyramid in Giza, Egypt. Originally 755 feet tall (now 481 feet), it is considered one of the Seven Wonders of the Ancient World.

2166-1991 BC

The life of Abraham. God's covenant with Abraham establishes the Israelites as his chosen people.

2066 BC

Isaac, Abraham's son is born.

2006 BC

Jacob, Isaac's son, is born right after his twin brother, Esau. God later renames Jacob Israel. Jacob becomes the father of the twelve tribes of the nation of Israel.

c. 1971 BC

The Temple of Amun, the Egyptian false god of the sun, is built by Pharaoh Senusret I in Karnak, Egypt. The Karnak Temple Complex is used daily for over 1,700 years.

1915 BC

Joseph is born to Jacob and his wife, Rachel.

1886 BC

Isaac dies at 180 years old.

c. 1884 BC

Joseph becomes Egypt's second-in-command after being sold into slavery by his brothers.

c. 1876 BC

Perhaps the date that God brought Jacob's family to Goshen, Egypt, through Joseph.

1859 BC

Jacob dies in Goshen, after seventeen years in Egypt. He is 147 years old when he dies.

1805 BC

Joseph dies in Egypt at 110 years old. Joseph makes his brothers swear they will take his bones with them when God leads them out of Egypt.

c. 1750 BC

King Hammurabi rules Babylon and writes the Code of Hammurabi, 282 laws carved in stone. Moses would have studied this law code during his education in Egypt.

1570-1293 BC

The 18th Dynasty of Egypt is the strongest period of rule for Ancient Egypt.

1595 BC

The Hittites defeat Babylon.

c. 1570-1070 BC

The New Kingdom in Egypt. Thebes (now Luxor) was the capitol of Egypt at the time. The temples of Luxor and Karnak were located in the city, with the Valley of the Kings burial ground just three miles outside the city.

1526 BC

Moses is born. His mother hides him in a basket in the Nile where the Pharaoh's daughter bathes. Pharaoh's daughter adopts Moses.

1504-1453 BC

Pharaoh Thutmose III reigns over Egypt. A tomb painting for his prime minister, Rehkmire, shows foreigners making bricks. Thutmose III expands his empire into Canaan.

1504-1483 BC

Hatshepsut rules as the only female Pharaoh. Some people think Hatshepsut may have been Moses' adoptive mother.

c. 1453-1425 BC

Pharaoh Amenhotep II reigns over Egypt. The early date for the Exodus would indicate that Amenhotep II was the Pharaoh of the Exodus. Scripture does not indicate that Pharaoh followed his army into the Red Sea.

1486 BC

Moses kills the Egyptian overseer. He flees Egypt and spends forty years in Midian.

c. 1450-1027 BC

The Shang Dynasty rules in China.

1446 BC

The Exodus happens, and Moses is eighty years old! The Israelites celebrate the first Passover and leave captivity in Egypt. This is the early date for the Exodus.

- The people bring the bones of Joseph out of Egypt.
- God gives instructions for the tabernacle and the Israelites construct the portable temple.

1446-1445 BC

The Israelites camp at Mount Sinai, where God gives them the Law. They make and worship the golden calf, sinning terribly.

1446-1406 BC

The Israelites remain in the wilderness.

1406 BC

Moses dies at 120 years of age. Joshua leads the Israelites as they begin their conquest of Canaan.

c. 1208 BC

Pharaoh Merneptah inscribes an account of his victory over ancient Libyans in stone. The Merneptah Stele mentions a battle against Israel in Canaan around 1230 BC. It is the oldest mention of Israel that we have, outside of the Bible.

c. 1200 BC

The Hittite Empire collapses. The Hittites had controlled territory from Turkey to parts of Syria and Lebanon.

c. 1164 BC

Egypt loses much of its power.

c. 966 BC

The Israelite Temple is finished and dedicated, built under Solomon, 480 years after the Exodus (1 Kings 6:1).

c. AD 30

Jesus is crucified. He is raised from the dead and ascends to heaven.

WORKS CONSULTED

Blaylock, Richard. "The Doctrine of Reprobation." The Gospel Coalition. https://www.thegospelcoalition.org/essay/doctrine-of-reprobation/. Accessed October 2022.

Boice, James Montgomery. *The Life of Moses: God's First Deliverer of Israel.* P&R Publishing, 2018.

Collins, John. "Miracles." The Gospel Coalition. https://www.thegospelcoalition.org/essay/miracles/. Accessed February 16, 2023.

Currid, John D. and David P. Barrett. *Crossway ESV Bible Atlas.* Crossway, 2010.

"Date of the Exodus." Evidence Unseen. https://www.evidenceunseen.com/date-of-the-Exodus/. Accessed October 2022.

Grudem, Wayne. *Systematic Theology: An Introduction to Biblical Doctrine.* Zondervan, 1995.

Hamilton, Adam. *Moses: In the Footsteps of the Reluctant Prophet.* Abingdon Press, 2017.

"How can I achieve victory in Jesus?" Got Questions Ministries. https://www.gotquestions.org/victory-in-Jesus.html. Accessed February 15, 2023.

Janzen, Mark D., Scott Stripling, James K. Hoffmeier, Peter Feinman, Gary A. Rendsburg, and Ronald Hendel. *Five Views on the Exodus: Historicity, Chronology, and Theological Implications.* Zondervan Academic, 2021.

Oliphant, Margaret. *The Atlas of the Ancient World: Charting the Great Civilizations of the Past.* Barnes & Noble Books, 1998.

Packer, J. I. *Knowing God*. InterVarsity Press, 2001.

Pink, Arthur. *The Attributes of God*. The New Christian Classics, 2018.

Rose Book of Bible Charts, Maps & Time Lines. Rose Publishing, 2010.

Rose Guide to the Tabernacle. Rose Publishing, 2016.

Sproul, R.C. "What is Providence?" Ligonier. https://www.ligonier.org/learn/articles/what-providence. Accessed February 15, 2023.

The ESV Study Bible™, ESV® Bible. Crossway, 2008.

Tozer, A.W. *The Attributes of God, Volume 1: A Journey into the Father's Heart*. WingSpread Publishers, 2007.

Tozer, A.W. *The Attributes of God, Volume 2: Deeper Into the Father's Heart*. WingSpread Publishers, 2007.

"What is divine providence?" Got Questions Ministries. https://www.gotquestions.org/divine-providence.html. Accessed February 15, 2023.

"What is the Shekinah glory?" Got Questions Ministries. https://www.gotquestions.org/shekinah-glory.html. Accessed February 15, 2023.

CHRISTIAN FOCUS PUBLICATIONS

CF4•K
*Because you're never
too young to know Jesus*

Christian Focus Publications publishes books for adults and children under its four main imprints: Christian Focus, CF4K, Mentor and Christian Heritage. Our books reflect our conviction that God's Word is reliable and Jesus is the way to know him, and live for ever with him.

Our children's publication list covers pre-school to early teens. We also publish personal and family devotional titles, biographies and inspirational stories that children will love.

From pre-school board books to teenage apologetics, we have it covered!

Christian Focus Publications Ltd,
Geanies House, Fearn, Ross-shire,
IV20 1TW, Scotland,
United Kingdom.
www.christianfocus.com